MID-LIFE

Written By:
Herbert Kavet

Illustrated By:
Martin Riskin

Manufactured in the United States of America

30 29 28 27 26 25 24 23 22 21 20 19 18 17 16 15 14 13 12 11 10 9 8 7 6 5 4 3 2 1

Ivory Tower Publishing Co., Inc.
125 Walnut St., Watertown, MA 02172
Telephone #: (617) 923-1111   Fax #: (617) 923-8839

MIDLIFE SEX IS COMPROMISING ON VACATIONS.

"WHY IS IT 98% OF MEN HAVE ORGASMS WHEN THEY SCREW AND ONLY 6% OF WOMEN DO?"
"WHO CARES?"

"MID-LIFE SEX IS ACCOMMODATING YOURSELF
TO YOUR SPOUSE'S PETS.

MIDLIFE SEX IS KNOWING WHEN YOU'RE NOT SATISFYING YOUR WIFE.

CLASS OF 1959
REUNION
"REMEMBER ME, LESTER, MELNIA PINSKER? WE USED TO DO IT BEHIND THE BATTING CAGE."

MID-LIFE SEX IS TAKING IT
ANY WAY YOU CAN GET IT.

MID-LIFE SEX IS BEING ABLE TO FIGURE OUT WHEN YOUR WIFE IS BEING UNFAITHFUL.

MID-LIFE SEX IS AGREEING ON ROOM TEMPERATURE.

MID-LIFE SEX IS TAKING THE GOOD SWAPS WITH THE BAD ONES AT A SWINGER'S CLUB.

MIDLIFE SEX IS BEING TIRED AFTER
A HARD DAY AT THE OFFICE.

MID-LIFE SEX IS A WORKING ACCOMMODATION
WITH FOUNDATION GARMENTS.

MID-LIFE SEX IS NEVER DOING IT MORE THAN ONCE WITH YOUR WIFE.

MID-LIFE SEX IS KIDS WHO NEED A DRINK BEFORE FALLING ASLEEP.

MID LIFE SEX IS SPENDING HOURS AND HOURS SEARCHING FOR NEW EROGENOUS ZONES.

MID-LIFE SEX IS HAVING AN ORGASM OVER
REALLY GOOD CHEESECAKE.

MID-LIFE SEX IS WORRYING ABOUT THE KIDS HEARING YOUR CLIMAX.

MID-LIFE SEX IS BEING ABLE TO DANCE REAL CLOSE
WITHOUT GETTING AN ERECTION.

MID-LIFE SEX IS REALIZING CERTAIN OUTFITS
ONLY WORK FOR 19 YEAR OLDS.

MIDLIFE SEX IS BEING ABLE TO VACATION
IN SOME REALLY EXOTIC PLACES.

MID-LIFE SEX IS KNOWING HOW TO GET RID OF YOUR PARTNER AFTERWARD.

"WE ONLY WORK ON MULTIPLE ORGASMS
ON WEEKENDS."
REPLACE
DIVOTS
17

MID LIFE SEX IS HAVING YOUR WIFE ALL AROUSED AFTER A FEW DRINKS.

MID-LIFE SEX IS HAVING YOUR KIDS
DISCOVER YOUR INTIMATE APPAREL COLLECTION.

MID-LIFE SEX IS RESIGNING YOURSELF TO EXCRUCIATINGLY UNCOMFORTABLE POSITIONS TO KEEP FROM WAKING YOUR MATE.

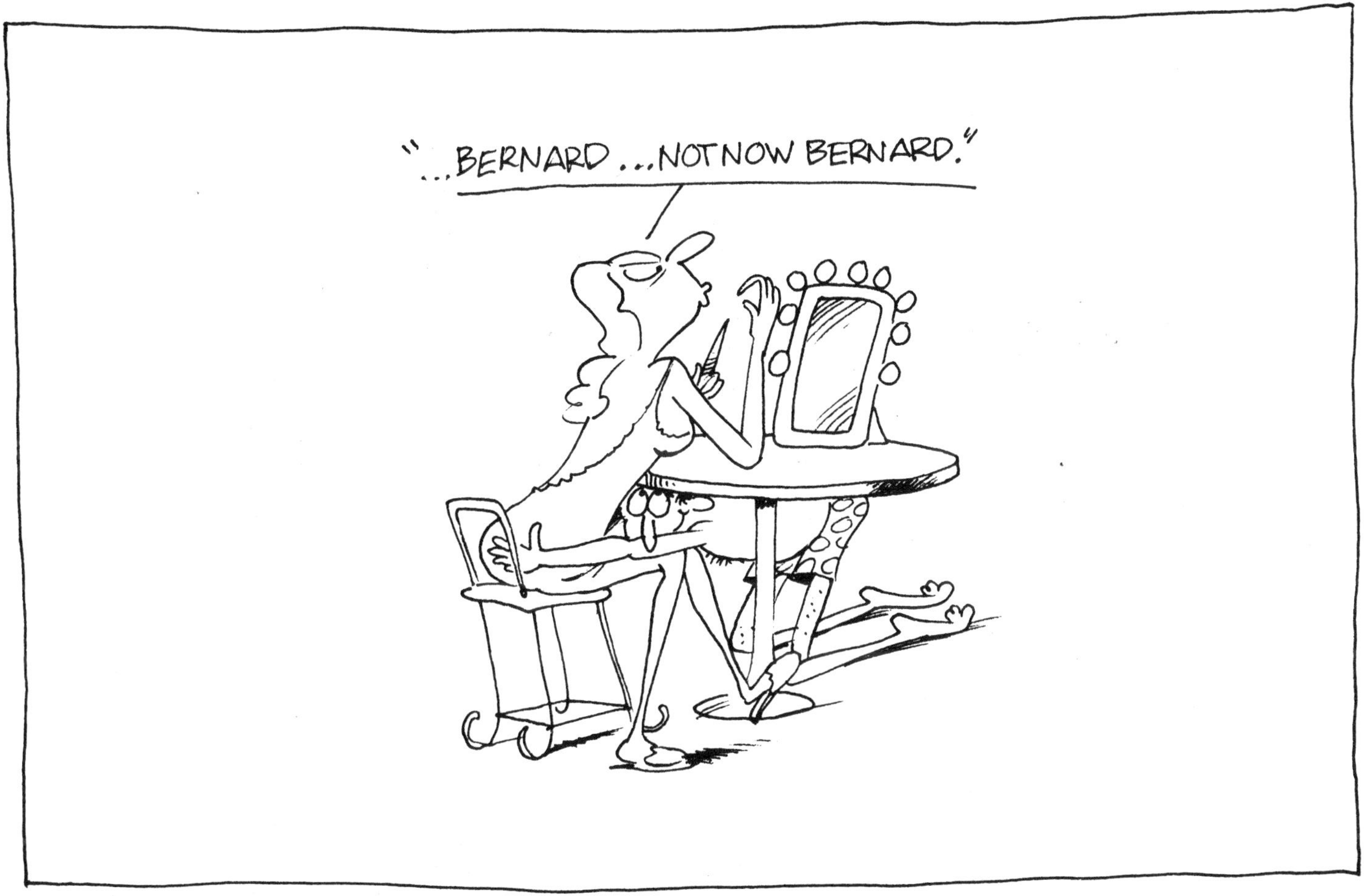
"...BERNARD ...NOT NOW BERNARD."

MID-LIFE SEX IS BEING TOLERANT OF FARTS
UNDER THE COVERS.

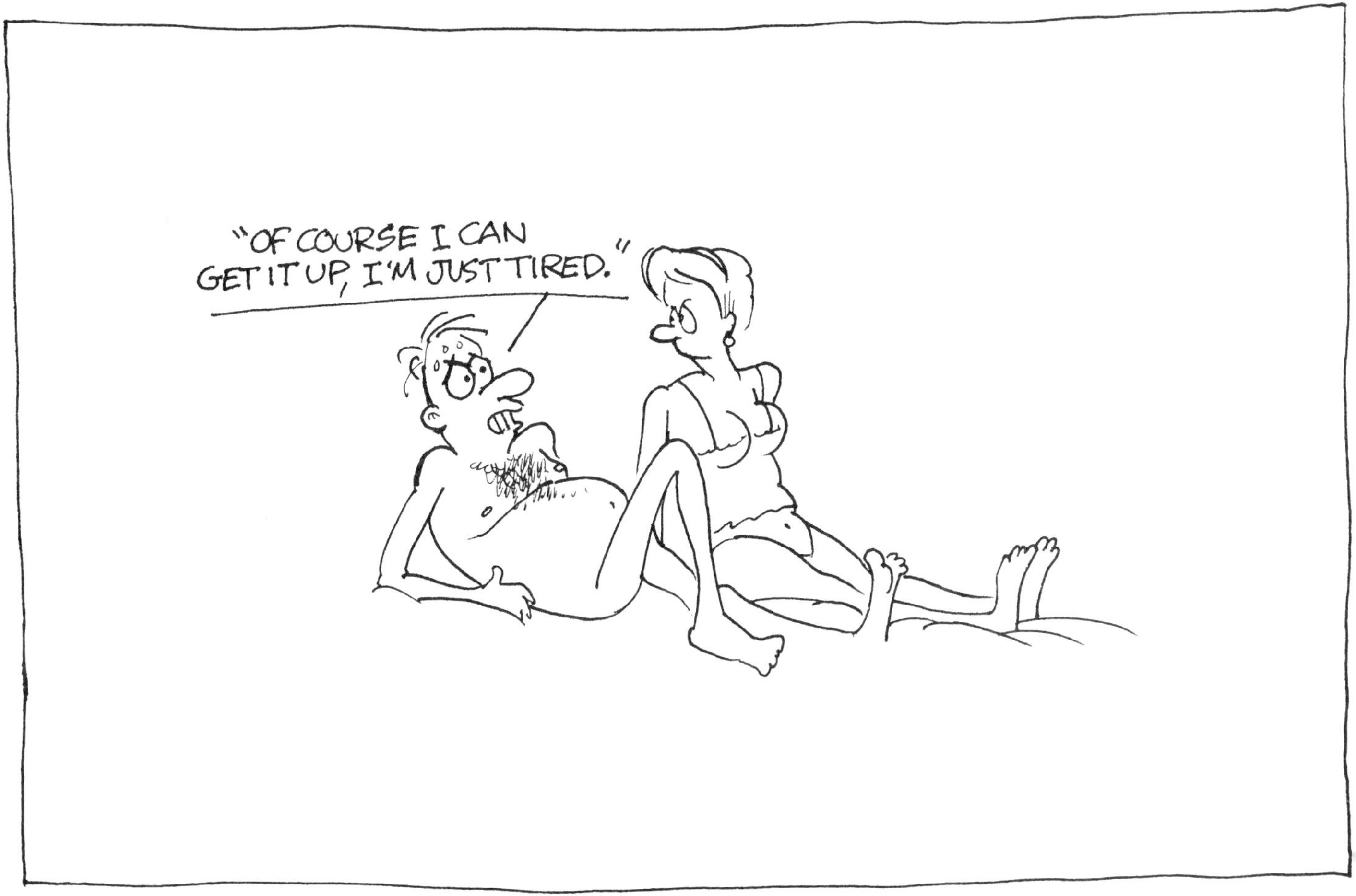
"OF COURSE I CAN GET IT UP, I'M JUST TIRED."

MID-LIFE SEX IS SOMETIMES WAITING UNTIL HALFTIME.

MID-LIFE SEX IS BEING REALLY APPRECIATED FOR AN ENTHUSIASTIC PERFORMANCE.

PINESNORT
BEACH

NUDE BATHING
ALLOWED

MID-LIFE SEX IS TALKING YOUR WIFE
INTO VISITING A NUDE BEACH.

MID-LIFE SEX IS 96% OF ALL YOUR
SEXUAL ACTIVITY TAKING PLACE IN BED.

MID-LIFE SEX IS HIDING SEX AIDS FROM THE KIDS.